# SOUTHERN STORIES AND SONGS

**POEMS**

Njanguma S. Momodu

**Sierra Leonean Writers Series**
Warima/Freetown/Accra
120 Kissy Road Freetown, Sierra Leone
Kofi Annan Avenue, North Legon, Accra, Ghana
Publisher: Prof. Osman Sankoh (Mallam O.)
publisher@sl-writers-series.org
www.sl-writers-series.org

**Southern Stories and Songs (Poems)**
Copyright © 2017 by Njanguma S. Momodu
All rights reserved.

ISBN: 978-9988-8743-0-8

Sierra Leonean Writers Series

## Dedication

To all the men, women, children and animals of the world who dare to take on the harassment of poverty; to the countless calloused hands that daily fight to feed the numerous mouths and fill the countless stomachs; to all the necks squashed in by the burdens on their heads; to all the brows beaten by the sweltering sun and drenched in beads of sweat; to all the large hearts and alert minds giving vent to voiceless lips; to all the grimy faces, muddled minds and shuffling feet stranded at the margins of society; to the spirit of the human family that continues to say 'no' to sweat shops, 'no' to mental slavery, 'no' to indentured slavery and all the unfair deals and indescribable vices that dehumanises our human family, I dedicate this work to you all.

## About the Collection

'Southern Stories and Songs' is a collection of fifty-two poems written during the month of Ramadan, reflecting on the various shades of poverty. The south in the title refers to the global south or the southern hemisphere, which is currently replete with poverty; the book, however, presents the south in two ways; on the one hand, it echoes the songs and stories of fatality, hopelessness, marginalisation, vulnerability and failed dreams; while on the other hand, it sings and narrate stories of hope; particularly of the galvanisation of the human family in their resilience and triumph over the adverse conditions of penury. There can be no better time that necessitates the discussion of the greatest blighter of lives in the south than now, when the millennium goals or targets of reducing poverty has catastrophically failed; at a time when all attempts of 'making poverty history' has proved glaringly disappointing; at a time when the global south continues to grovel in abject poverty; clearly there is a need for people to make sense of their lives and this book provides that fresh angle, which will, hopefully, teach the north a thing or two about poverty and its impact on: nature, the psyche of the poor and its implications for the sustainable future.

To provide a friendlier reading experience, this collection has been divided into seven sections or clusters. Cluster one: contains eighteen narrative poems or stories based on the theme of poverty and its impact on human lives, cult ure, politics, religion and nature; cluster two: contains sonnets on the theme of penury; cluster three: contains poems that explore the biases in power and how certain conflicts can make the situation of the poor worst; cluster four: looks at the assertiveness of the poor in the face of abject poverty; cluster five: looks at the education of the soul through suffering in order to attain enlightenment; cluster six: looks at the ability of man, animals and nature to motivate others in their trying needs and, finally, cluster seven: looks at the human conditions of hunger, crime etc and its impact on the marginalised in society. If only not to pre-empt reader's conclusions on each poem and spoil their enjoyment, a poem-by-poem summary has been provided at the back of the book, to indicate the intended breath of themes to be covered and provide a starting point for students and teachers who might want to use these poems for their poetry lessons.

## CONTENTS

Dedication, i
About the Collection, ii

### CLUSTER 1 Stories, 1

1. The Hawker, 2
2. Diamond Diggers, 4
3. The Pills of Pa Kumasi, 7
4. Death of a Doctor, 9
5. Usain Bolt in Sierra Leone, 11
6. The Pride of Pa Palma, 14
7. The Beggar, 16
8. The Phantom of Fasting, 18
9. Bra Samora and His Crocodile Shoe, 21
10. The Prodigal Son, 22
11. Bra Bockarie's Sacred Sac of Rice, 23
12. The Widow Who Married Her Church, 25
13. The Soul Whisperer, 27
14. The Man Who Sold Himself off on a Loan, 29
15. The Hypocrite, 32
16. Cookies to Heaven, 35
17. Dodger, 36
18. Chimney, 38

### CLUSTER: 2 Sonnets, 40

19. Job, 41
20. The Poverty Projects, 42
21. Ebola, 43
22. The Funeral of a Pauper, 44

### CLUSTER: 3 Power and conflict, 45

23. Cocoa Farmers, 46

24. The Sermon of a Church Mouse, 47
25. The Godhead of Alafia, 48
26. Commonwealth, 50
27. Wealth, the Creator of Poverty, 51
28. The Question of Heaven, 52
29. Rattitude, 53
30. Kono People, 55
31. Thank God My Daddy Is Not Poor, 57
32. Tax Slave, 58
33. Tsunami Monday, 59
34. Hammattan, 61

**CLUSTER: 4 Taking a stand or Assertion, 62**

35. The Countdown Steps Out of Poverty, 63
36. Spirit of a Family Home, 65
37. Hallamory, 67
38. Poverty, You Have Failed, 68
39. When Shall We Make Poverty History? 71

**CLUSTER: 5 Education and Enlightenment, 74**

40. The Maths of Poverty, 75
41. Poverty, 78
42. The Soul Man, 80
43. Lightmare, 82

**CLUSTER: 6 Motivation and Nature, 85**

44. Songs of the Southern Stoics, 86
45. Rich and Poor, 89
46. If, 91
47. A Song of a Southern Son, 93
48. Lullaby, 95
49. They're Not Our God, 96

**CLUSTER: 7 Human Conditions, 97**

50. Hunger, 98
51. Poverty Is Not a Crime, 100
52. Poverty – an Armed Robber, 101
53. The Man-Eater of the South, 102

Poems: one, or two, line summary, 105
About the author, 108

# CLUSTER ONE
## Stories

## 1. The Hawker

On God's day of rest, a barefooted boy
hawks, while the tides travel the world;
he hawks, while the sun surveys the skies;
he hawks, while snakes snore
in subterranean soils;
he hawks, hawks and hawks.

PURE WATER! He calls
like the heart beating the drums of life
PURE WATER! He calls
until a careering car kicks him
flying…
Saucer stains with splatter of redness.

At once, a mournful dust rises
like the clamour of protesting neighbours,
slumps to the soil and grovels on ground
in mourning…
Satchel of plastic water, strewing the streets
splits into sprinklers

      The car magics into mystery…

To the bated breaths
the sprawled boy spasms
to the gapping gazes, he stills.
His nose and mouth spumes
with redness
on that cursed altar
of 'making ends meet'
with harshness.

His writhing eyes all-rapt
at the beckoning fingers of angels
      his tender face
not lined with twinges of pain
cracks in a seraphic smile

to the muffled grunts of his mother
his smile sings relief from drudgery
in the sidling, mysterious driver's
steps, a fear of reprisals, prison and pain

to the wet faces of by-standers
he waves;
to being a beast of burden
he waves;
to the alters of want
his soul waves
to hunger and mockery. he waves.

Would he had grown to be guarded
or be a guard? He smiles…
Would he had been tutored
or be self-tutored? Silence….
Would he have been a prince
or a chaperon? He smiles.
In the eyes of the sun, his sweat, his smile.
In the jaws of the earth; his tears, his blood,
his flesh…

## 2. Diamond Diggers

There was our fair-skinned
Prof-Sheikh who carried cars
and rent-free mansions
in his primary school teacher's head…

He ditched the duster
for the dung
swapped pen and paltry pay
for a pickaxe
children's snotty noses
for the promises of the peat
muddied his maroon skin
with sand and shingles
    searched for stones
in murky streams

in place of scholarship
shovels and shakers
in place of his wife; wistful wishes
in place of his child
his cry for crystal white

it took a police whistle
to whoosh him into plunging,
took some guttering, gurgling, reeling
for him to quench
in the greedy guts of the Moiday River

Stiff. Palled. Daddy…
His son's startled stare said it all:
why would his dad's play
at 'mummies and zombies'
make his mum whimper?

There was San-San-Boy-Sam
whose years of bending double
turned his back into
a Chinese crockery
kinked, glued, taped
nailed, plated and hinged
    No longer nimble
in his thrust of hip
he recalls, with fondness,
his phallic Everest
beside the body warmers of his youth

Now though, his legs
all waterlogged
about his creaky bones
shoots pains and cramps.
Legs that once eluded
leeches, mites' bites and police chase
now measures his steps
after a palsy tap of staff…
palms: once oiled with hard currencies
now cracked and calloused;
limbs: droopy, rusty; no more robotic…

Yet a whisper of a fluky find
of a gigantic gem
gels the wrinkly thread
on his brow
straightens his back
unclenches his pain-tightened jaws
contortions
off his cherubic-face!

Njanguma S. Momodu

How about X?
How did he shell our Eden city?

With dynamites
he droned hymnals in churches
and desecrated shrines
with kimberlite
he shook statuettes
made strictures in walls of mosques.
With semtex,
he opened waterways
and flooded plantations

he moulded mountains
closed off motorways
dug craters in the gut of the city
he bull-dozed ditties
and dug out chorus of mosquitoes…

That's enough!

*Moiday: a river in the Kono District of Sierra Leone*
*Prof: shorten form for professor*
*Sheikh: is Arabic for teacher*

## 3. The Pills of Pa Kumasi

When his elephantine efforts
yielded into a mere molehill
he thought of buying a gun
to gun down hunger
and bring back his life's thrills...

What week went by
when the wedding songs
of neighbours didn't drone out
'the sermon on the mount' in his ears?

When his pay packet
failed to fend off the bailiff
the landlord and the bank
he thought up a sturdy string
to tidy things up and keep his rank.

What letter didn't remind him
of unpaid school fees?
What hospital calls didn't
threaten him for unpaid bills?

When his hands refused
to bring back home the steak
for his many yawing mouths,
refused to fill
the nine-month's hollow
hunger had dug out
in his mother's stomach,
      he found inviting
a carving knife
that must sever off
the uselessness of his hands...

When didn't he slouch
where other shoulders
stayed straightened
bowed where all heads
were held high
wide-eyed in the cosy house of snores
fidgety on God's day of rest?


When his lips
which once confessed love
suddenly stretched into lies and laments
his eyes look past
the beauty he once adored
and showered with compliments
      he thought of plunging
into the dark depths
to bring back his merriments

But when cumulus clouds
blotted out the sun
and the morrow
promised him thunder
the proverbial straw had
broken his camel's back
So long, for his desert crossing…
With all his joys put asunder

So he plied himself with pills
on an empty tummy
grovelled, writhed, sprawled
off the gun, the string, the knife…

## 4. Death of a Doctor

When Papa's sleep made me
a father to my brother
and Mama's silence made me
a mother to my younger brother
we survived.

When each sun saw me as a learner
and my brother's teacher
the evening, a tuck-shop trader;
the night, a Lebanese gate-keeper
we survived.

When my sales and pay fell short
of my W.A.E.C fees
the Darwin that died in me
rose as Mendel in him
we survived.

With nails in my palm, cross on my back
thorns to my brow
my nights of Hook's law
became his day of pickled frogs…
We survived.

Didn't the tigress hunt
to feed her hungry cubs?
Didn't the tireless heart
beat to keep the body alive?
We survived.
Didn't the mantis offer himself
to his mate as a grub?
Didn't mothers starve of sleep
for their child to survive?
We survived.

With my back to periodic tables
and his head drowned in labs
I scrubbed; he swatted; we prayed
till our knees swelled with scabs
We survived.

With me in overalls
and him in a white long coat
the light that died in me
had risen in him for a toast
We survived.

With me on a bier
and him with a stethoscope
my brother, my father,
my doctor had given me hope
We survived! We survived!

1. *W.A.E.C. West African Examination Council*

## 5. Usain Bolt in Sierra Leone

Our thin bones said that
we shouldn't have run.
Why? Because the town clerk's son
had long won
even before the referee's whistle
had gone

Unlike us who breakfasted
on a left-over rice
he had tea with Carnation milk
a fat slice of bread with butter
he had eggs and cress
unlike us whose lunch
 was to brace our churning tummies
his dinner was a bowl
 of chicken salad, a tiny rice with green peas
capped with meat in gravy
unlike our rice
which was as dry as a bone.

Our pale faces said that
we shouldn't have run
Why? Because the town clerk's son
had long won
even before the 'unto your mark'
had gone

Against his bearded face
our bald, sweaty chins.
Against our dwarfish cut; a Samson
against our thin bones
the legs of a bison
Against our tortoise pace; an Achillean leap
'on' and 'off' the pitch

he was of the big boy's league...

Our weak voices said that
we shouldn't have run
Why? Because the town clerk's son
had long won
even before the referee's prompt of 'steady'
had gone

unlike shallow eyes who read
by candle and kerosene lamps
he'd read by halogen lights
or by his table lamp
unlike us who suffered
from 'B' deficiency
he'd swallowed vitamin pills
for maximum efficiency
unlike us who had to tutor
ourselves in mathematics
he'd paid-teachers to give him
extra tuition in physics

why did we race
where the likes of us
shouldn't have run?

Unlike bland biceps who used
stools and stones as weights
he'd a gym and trainers
to take him to the heights
so, he sprinted with the legs
of Bolt and won
unlike our feeble feet
that fell, fainted and failed
his was the flash of fist

beyond the touchline
unlike ashen hearts
who gulped for breath and zest
his was a lightning
that droned with loud rolls
sadly, our bloodless veins
had said that we shouldn't have run
because the town clerk's son long had
the ready, the steady and the all go!

## 6. The Pride of Pa Palma

Poverty, they say, is a curse
 except for Pa Palma
because when his palm wine sales
didn't buy him scented soaps
he made black soap from banana husk
to wash his corduroy
 when his bush meat sale
didn't buy him vegetable oil
he strained oil from palm kernel
 to oil his *tolla soup*
 when his fish sale
didn't buy him a crocodile shoe
he designed sandals from disused tyres
 to save his sole from sores

Poverty, they say, is a curse
except for Pa Palma
because when his bank balance
didn't buy him Gucci clothes
he wove himself a *ronko*
and patterned his *gara* gown
 when his odd jobs
didn't buy him a bag of rice
he made yebeh from cassava
to chase off his hunger
 when his wife's *attire* sales
didn't buy them electric iron
they put charcoal in iron goose
and ironed creases out of his *agbada*

Poverty, they say, is a curse
except for Pa Palma
because to each speck of dirt

his broom; to grease or grim, his soap
to rank bushes his machete
to swelled gutters his shovel
to mosquitoes and typhoid fever
he had long waved bye bye!

Poverty, they say, is a curse
except for Pa Palma
because to his wife's heart
his love; to all fights, his apologies,
to all troubles his caution
and to divorce? He had long
waved goodbye!

Poverty, they say, is a curse
except for Pa Palma
because his kitty contained
Abib's school fees; from his osusu
pay out, his adult education fees
and to ignorance and illiteracy?
Mr and Mrs Palma and Abib
had long waved bye bye!

Foot note:
1.Tolla soup is a seed grounded in a brownish powder. It is slimy like okra.
2.Ronk: is cotton cloth soaked in brown dye, often worn by titled men of clans as a sign of authority
3.Gara gown is a curtain material dyed with patterned colours
4. Yebeh is a porridge of cocoa, cassava, yam, banana and potato
5.Agbadah is a flowing gown worn for special occasions such as a wedding
6. Osusu is a cooperative bank in which the participants take turns at receiving monthly pay-outs
7. Attire: is a tea joint that sells non-alcoholic drinks.

## 7. The Beggar

His feet wore well-worn crepe
for shoes.
Not one for dancing

His thin bones wore baggy rags
for clothes.
Not one for bluffing

His face wore yearnings
for eyes.
Long done with crying

His legs wore wet breeches
for trousers.
Not one for officiating

Robbed of a name he pleaded
in God's name.
Robbed of parents he adopted
his benefactors
as his Mum and dad'

'In God's name I greet you, sir'
he croaked,
'I beg of you, ma; please give me
water to drink…'
An icy tutik bottle, to loosen
the grip of thirst on his throat.
'In God's name' he pleaded, 'open it
for me sir and hold it to my mouth…'
'What?' I scoffed, incensed with his audacity.
But
In the socket of my eyes,

made blurred
with the drunkenness of annoyance,
a touch shone on his ghastly scar,
his half-hacked hand,
a flash of a mattock, of machete,
       a dangling white-elephant.
In my slurred speech of spite
a tiny voice of reason spoke
of his porcelain hand,
in a land of veined hands
digging with hoes.
Within the room of my guilt
I learned: of a hunter's timely shot
that had saved him
of his stay at 'The House of Light'
on a rock, in a city called Freetown…
What were his chances of a gainful job
in a land where blood-filled-hands
were idle?


Learnt:
of his need for caution,
for care and a bit of
CHANGE…


1.   *Tutik: bottled water*

## 8. The Phantom of Fasting

And the fox within Sanusi
bided him to trail in its steps
for a full moon's trek
from the bustle of Freetown
into the wilderness of Jesus
in the desert of Mohammed
in the gutters of Siddhartha, the prince.

'In vain shall a man part a sound
from a voice. Heat from fire,
chills from the harmattan
a shadow from a body; all your life,
you'd carried me in you;
take my bidding and you're right,
act on your own and you err,
best we unite…'

Thus, the Solomon in Sanusi
taught him songs of emptiness:
of Matorki, the poor wine seller,
whose soul asked him: to fetch
an empty oil can; bore a hole
in the can's hollow; place old
broken files over the hole;
glued down some sticks
at the can's edge, hang rattles to it
welcome to the birth of the Kongoma
let it sing of man's emptiness…

The wine seller's fingers
plucked the files:
One piped in bass; another in a tenor
then soprano, then contralto

then alto but together
they sang of their freedom
from rust.

The empty can sang
of its joys of being useful
the rattle and its ball bearing
the can, the file, the rattle
lunged a nostalgic note
of being in the soil as ore again.

The spirit of fasting asked Sanusi
'What are you emptied of?
Is it of food, grudges, envy,
Jealousy, anger, hunger or hatred?
Wisdom is my song, he said,
but what songs do you sing?
Are they longings for peace
or long life; unity or heaven?
What thoughts do you have?
Are they of wealth? Or Salamatu?,
or of poor widows and orphans?

And the spirit said 'imagine a chopped
oak trunk chiselled into a TOMTOM.
Its top side sealed with a hide of deer
a hide free of its flesh; free of its bones
the oak hollowed as reed, stripped
of its back, squeezed of its sap
thus, as a duo; the hide and oak sang:
the hide sang of its family
the gambolling in the wild
the oak sang of longevity
the calmness by noontide

Next, the soul gave Sanusi
the scenario of a palm tree
whose side bore a deep wound,
a hollow that wept of wine,
only the wine was a tear of emptiness,
a song that induced the mind
to relaxation and sleep
its tears were for its failure
to touch the blue skies.
What tears do you shed
that do not intoxicate the mind
but induces the heart to sleep,
the soul to relaxation?

Thus ended the first of day of fasting…



*1.   Harmattan: cold westerly winds that blow across sub-Saharan Africa form November to February*
*2.   Tomtom: a drum*
*3.   Kongoma: a plucking instrument made of old can or canister, gallon or container.*

## 9.  Bra Samora and His Crocodile Shoe

Soap suds might soak me soggy
and hard bristle might brush me lustreless
but wherever he goes, I go.

His treks might bore holes in my sole
and puddles in potholes might sip inside of me
but wherever he goes, I go.

His job search might have worn me thin
and stones might scratch and bleed my nose
but wherever he goes, I go.

My heels might be laden with a cobbler's nail
and my sides chipped and lopsided
but wherever he goes, I go.

I might be soiled with grime or shoe polish
my inside clammy with sweat
but wherever he goes, I go.

I might stink to high heaven like a skunk
with my leather matching none of his ragged suits
but wherever he goes, I go.

He might neither have the money to replace me
nor the desire to bin his one and only love
hence, wherever he goes, I go.


1.   Bra: krio for brother - reserved for someone usually older than you as a mark of respect.

## 10. The Prodigal Son

The prodigal son is back
for goats, rice and more money
back after crippling our livestock
and reserve of honey

he puffs and throws
the tsunami of tantrums
huff, despite being the sole
survivor of the fiercest storm

he calls our house a hovel
and a dilapidated shack
pretends his loud music didn't
cause all these cracks

he moans at the lack
of food and grubs to bite
pretends he didn't bury
wasted food in landfilled sites

he yearns to see
the gazelle and the noble impala
bluffs his hunting parties
didn't wipe them with their Berettas

he says our hut is the dankest
of the Sahara desert
professed his factory fumes
didn't cause the dearth

he cries of mosquito bites
and bouts of diarrhoea
acts as if he didn't refuge to fund
our clean water and vaccine for malaria…

## 11. Bra Bockarie's Sacred Sack of Rice

In the place of pictures
statuettes and trophies
sat a small sack of rice
on a mantelpiece flanked
by candles and a censer
in the sanctum of his room.

Rather than Ramatu's face
at dawn
the first thing he beheld
was that sack
rather than peck
little Mimi's jaws
he would peck
the sack a good night kiss.

Once, he nearly filed
for divorce, rather than lose his altar
to the pantry
and when his wife, who saw things
in neat boxes, dared him
to keep the sack and loose her
 he was silent. Thick silence…

that helped her to her pillows
as she stormed out of his shrine
to her room
to shut out the rains and loud storms…

Silence, a thick silence
that sang of the sack
as the wall of China
loomed against the spectre
of a thin-boned child

(of his childhood)
ravenously choking on
a pinch of rice capped
with a sauce laced
with scotch bonnet pepper.
It took six litres of water
 to douse its fiery fires
nearly drowned his lungs
 and singed livers…

Silence. Thick silence
that spoke of a war
and a stooped seventy-seven-year-old
resting on a stick,
 who'd gobbled up fear,
 loneliness and pride.
So drunk on hunger
that he'd begged food
from armed rebels
but the rebels only felt
the chills and saw neither paleness
nor heard his whispers… shhhh!

Silence. Thick silence
that sang about a sack of bones
 his father's, he'd long buried
Sack of sacrifices to end
his line's curses of hunger
Sack of atonement to his past
 with its curses of son and father
Sack, as a vault, bulging with fear,
guilt, pains and curses of hunger.

## 12. The Widow Who Married Her Church

I must marry my late husband's younger brother
they said; because, our tradition said so; granted;
tradition, they said, led our daily steps, granted;
but do they know *who* leads my heart and mind?

Tradition, they said, was mightier than everyone
it neither lies nor pains; always fair and never bias
granted; but didn't it lie when it married me off
to a layabout and a drunk? How was that ever fair?

If I didn't marry their choice, our elders insisted,
I must leave the house but without my children,
granted; but why mustn't I keep what I'd toiled
to build; why leave with my late husband's name?

When he drowned his soul in alcohol, we drowned
when his vices creamed off my profit, we starved;
in his debts, we choked; at court cases, we cowed
who said that tradition was fair and never pained?

But for my church's saving grace, we would've died
from the thorns of a drunk in the flesh of my marriage
unlike me, sisi Petti chose her grown sons over their
lecherous uncles as guardians. How was she wrong?

I mustn't choose, they said, my children as guardians
because tradition said it was an abomination, granted;
but if tradition was fair, why shouldn't I choose friends
who shared my smoke, fires and tears; my loyal sons?

Our elders were wise and considerate, they said, granted;
but what was wise in making me homeless and destitute?
What was wise in forcing my heart in the jaws of a vice?
What's wrong with the church being my sole guardian?

1. *Sisi*: Madam. A term to show rank or respect.

## 13. The Soul Whisperer

On the gravelled concourse
of a muunku- market
where wide tyres reverses
in his snoring head
splutters the driver's mate's brains
into a pinkish gooey paste
and in that red puddle, of congealed redness
strewing the sun-drenched soil
spirals the soul of his spilled blood
singing of an altar of sand laid with a lamb
in his prime, as an atonement
to end his line's scourge of poverty
 there he is

in countless gawping eyes
in that clamouring crowd ringing
about that juggernaut
where the soul of his heart carols
his end of fear: fear of ritual killers
snatching orchids off market tables
I smell and feel him
in the rapt gaze of the sun

and in every watery eye
and to every dropped lip
in that hurdled crowd,
the soul of his squashed lips
pipes of his wish to console
those who mourn;
console his mother's gulping heart
apologises for his abrupt halt
to his intrepid walk on a tightrope

'Tell my boss,' he sings, '
that I forgive him…
for corking his ears to my bide
of good night…'
If only
he'd toned down his music,
hadn't plied himself with reef
and heady rum, he would have heard
his wish of sleeping
under the Fuso truck.

Amid that bustle and chaotic din
in the admixture of thick
fish stench and putrid gutters
the soul of his slushy brain croons
of his failed dreams
of limbs too still
to once more step on the tailgates
of hands too stiff
to ever take the steering wheels
of words too muted
to fill the void his father left
of a heart too inert
to care for a greying mother
of a soul too rash
to inhabit his hollowed turf.


1. Muuku: illiterate.

## 14. The Man Who Sold Himself off on a Loan

Under a thatched rafter
of a well-kept house
shone a mound
whose hollowed inside sang
to me about the soul of a farm-hand.

Sang of a time
when the late man's life
had glided past noontide
when his twilight
was about to usher in his dusk.

Carolled of him looking
back with a pang of regret
through squinted eyes
with a hint of quilt
as he mused upon
his youthful vagrancy
mused upon
his generational penury
how near his twilight
he was none the better:
for where others boasted
of mansions
as products of their youth
he was only too grateful
to his grandfather
for the safety
of his ramshackle house
where his age mates
gave alimony; he lived off
the largess of others
where the houses
of his equals echoed with

play-sounds of children
he'd remained a coveter
of others' wives; a helper
to countless childless unions
never once thought of a child
to bear his name
until that haunting death wish:

'Look for your father'
she'd croaked.

He sang of a past playing
havoc on his mind
of a young man
from his loins: same pate,
same stoutness,
same stature, carbon copy
of his voice,
spitting image of his carriage
crooned of rumours
of his son in search of him
and how he -a grey father-
had traced the seeker
to a farming village
where he'd pledged himself
on loan as a farming hand.

His payment? To keep
his identity secret, from his son
hummed of how
he couldn't bear to wake old evils.
Sang of his wish
of a befitting burial
when he'd joined the legion of silence.

He sang of the dusk of his life
how smiles
had gathered on his face
how his lips
had piped for his feet
threading the same
outdoor dust as his son
    regaled of furrows
straightened off his brow
sang of the spring's return
of his son's handshakes
stirring his ebbing life
    sang of how
his smile shone through dust
how his smile dried the raining tears
how his soul rang
through the thickening silence.

## 15. The Hypocrite

Her feet might've longed
for the soils of her native home
but she'd dared her toes
an inch on that laterite path
and she'd hitched her sole dry
of its yearnings.

The ditties of her home might've
sang out for her embrace and
her blood line might've beckoned
for a peck but she'd tuned up
her music to drone out
the beseeching songs.

Then her lips would suck
her teeth at the raggedy cradle
her mind would curse her roots…
still, the palimpsest of shadows
lingered on.

Next, she'd replaced
her surname with a Christian name
adopted a pompous American drawl
which besieged her rural tongue
but her native tongue would sing
of its release from chains
tying it to the back of her neck
its emotive guttural pleas would trip
her American accent
but she'd swallow deep
resolved: 'more elocution lessons'
she'd clipped her finger
'and all traces of that bush tongue is gone'

still the native tongue would sing
much to her dislike.

Next, she'd call herself
a mermaid fit only for the royals
only the marine kingdom
saw a human beneath the bleached
veneer of her skin; a weak vision
in her contact lenses; fake nails
for her fangs, and the royals saw
neither a trace of royal blood
in her veins nor any dainty pose
in her carriage.

That she hated herself
she refused to own up
So, she spited all her earthly ties
built herself a palace in the high heavens
but through the bolted gates
of her ivory nest, a voice
from a dust track would sing
calling her to a mud-brick
tumbled-down homestead
flanked by the outstretched hands
of her slovenly-dressed parents
but she'd dodge; stymied, clench
fisted, stiff-lipped as she'd down
glasses of heady rum
to dull the glare of their image.

In her buffoonery, she'd adopted
the senator as her father; declared
her mother late; claimed to be engaged
to the president's son; but, then,
the rooster crowed
when the president's son

saw beneath her Brazilian wig
a hair cropped by a cotton cushion
squashed by butt-ends of buckets
of water from a village stream
smelled a whiff of musky earth
in her Parisian perfume
perceived perched locust and snails
fried in fat oil on her vermillion lips.
 He named her class
and her crest farrowed and fell
the razor-sharp claws reaped
its sacking and out leapt the cat
and out tumbled brimstone
when her parents showed
unannounced at her university-hostel
accused her of estrangement,
ungratefulness and falsity…

Then there was the senator's visit
and his vehement denial
of any blood ties with her
forced, out of her, a solemn wish:
but there was no earthly chasm
to gobble her up.
Ditched
but for the song of her roots
that lingered on…

## 16. Cookies to Heaven

Sad how Scottie comes and claws at my twenty years of regular tips
gobbles my joy, shares madam's bed, crawls beside her on the sofa
whereas I, Bernadine, must stand at ease or always on point duty
brace up to fight rude visitors or wield my knife at mean burglars.

For forty years, the Romains didn't lose a pin or a strand of hair
yet it's Scottie that gets the treats, the peck and the silver star
unlike Scottie who fetches some twigs, balls and paper, I've to
fetch water, bundles of wood, sacks of rice and polish madam's car.

Yet it's Scottie this, good girl that! Of course, it's very true,
that I'm too grey to be noticed, no bushy tail to fondly wag
won't dare doze off or snore; talk less of drooling my tongue
to lick madam's velvety face or I'll be tossed off like a rag.

It's true I can't afford a deluxe shampoo, a vet or constipation
neither paws to hop in madam's lap nor can I afford a china
I might be ragged for her Rover's front seat, too hoarse to be heard
but I sure must shuffle on a stick for a crown to feed my daughters.

Pedigree chum for Scottie; paltry wages for good Old Bernadine
but today Scottie must eat lovely cookies to sweet heaven
for clawing my wages, it must go for Yinka and Zenab must learn
I must hush this rude barking, get my tips and peace of mind.

## 17. The Dodgers

'Ten days of grace for the thief,'
says the sage,
'a day of reckoning for the owner.'
Thus, his foxiness at fare-dodging
ended the day his frantic peeping
out doors and windows ended.
The under-collars
of his smart suit smothered
the day the fines were slapped at his face…
      the air of invisibility
and his 'hide and seek' ended
the day the CCTV cameras
called up the police
his flimsy excuses
of a poor memory ended
the day the cuff manacled his wrist
his pocket, puffed with coins
and notes, failed him,
the day his thrill turned into an ordeal
the iron centipede bound
to Cockfosters failed him
the day it shuttled to cock-fraudsters
the edging of seats
and gadding from coach-to- coach ended
the day the suspicious glances
over his shoulders ended
the probing of commuters
and alighters ended
the day the civilian-dressed conducted
out-foxed him
      shuffling of feet
and palpitation of his heart ended
the day those scarlet letters

marked him out for shame…

In the wake of that tiny eye
that beheld with its tiny periscope
the birth of that distant star
    in the wake of finding
that pin in that hay stack
those hounds fishing out
their quarry from its bolthole
that crucial antidote
to that terminal illness
in the wake of Goliath
meeting its nemesis
    I thought of the countless
dodgers of my youth:
poor tenants evading
overzealous landlords
    illicit miners
circumventing police officers
cash-strapped citizens
bypassing permit inspectors
    drivers dodging
licence collectors
okada drivers dodging
 checkpoints
dodgers dodging with guilt
never dodging to thrill themselves.

1. Okada is a motor bike used as a taxi service.

## 18. Chimney

'Long before he died,' Grandpa lamented,
'your Uncle Chimney was a suicide' he said
'to fill the void of joblessness in his heart,
he swigged forty-sticks of fags and, like a
dragon, he puffed out belching fumes from
his nostrils; hence, his name, Chimney.'

'So, never you smoke, my child,' he warned,
'or do you want bags under your eyes,
do you want to burn the garden in you?'
'Nup, Grandpa.'
'Do you want brown, tobacco fingers?
Do you want to pollute the seat of the soul,
the chamber of the conscience?'
'Nup...'
'Do you want black tartars on your teeth,
beer breath, break the poor dentist's scalpel
or blind the eye of God in you?'
'No Grandpa.'

Grandpa went on, 'Your Uncle Chimney hated
our dentist, cause he called your uncle's breath
a cesspit. He hated his surgeon, cause he
butchered him to get rid of a clot on his liver
and the tar on his lungs.' Grandpa said.

'Uncle Chimney wasn't ugly, but poverty
drew his face and smoking made him an ogre.
Nicotine made him a slave of Marlborough
and sweet-menthol singed his liver and lungs.

The claws of chemicals in each stick so scratched
his throat that he croaked. Fumes of depression

so leeched his juices that he leaned, all gaunt.
Then eventually' he said, 'cigarettes gave him
a cough then asthma, then oedema then cancer.'

He said Uncle Chimney had a triple bypass, tubes
everywhere; but the radio and chemo didn't cure him.
Doctor said that my uncle was terminal and I guess
he didn't want to go to terminal five, so he stole off
in his sleep. 'he'd never come back,' Grandpa said.

# CLUSTER TWO:
Sonnets

## 19. Job

With a child's faithfulness; the sun, Job did revere
with a dog's dedication; her halo of noon, he did extol
with a child's devotion; her horizon, he did adore
like nature's order; her resplendent rays, he did exalt...
    off his ties and stead, upon her shrine alone, he did retire
bare of stately robes, to her service alone, he did aspire
her rise; his chant; her high-noon, his dance; her set, his empire...
What possession did he not trade in to sate her heart's desires?

Yet by day, her billion spears; upon his soul, did highlight
by night, her strangling hold of heat, to his neck, did clutch.
To his gulping throat, no water; to his groping hands, no light...
his candour ditched; his efforts- of praise – waved as a staled broth
by a sun that sores; make bilious his blood and set his life alight;
pallor his skin, shallows his breath and smites him with all her might...

## 20. The Poverty Projects

In crack, whore houses and rum stores of the shanty
life leads our souls before the sword of depravity
where poverty shoots missiles of envy and rivalry
crushing tall hopes upon our fields of penury.
but a robin's song serenades in such soprano
that rallies our heads to bear our horns as hawkers
farmers and tailors, carpenters and drivers, nurses and teachers
all whistling with thrills as sweets as a robin's alto.

O rainbow to pains and anthem to laughter
who rouses war-wearied bodies to pious orders
why not thrill our hollowed hearts with a spring
that sheds it wrath, tosses off anger and wings
in all, as it plods my soul to his thunderous pen
saddles me on winged-words, contentment bound, to Eden?

## 21. Funeral of a Pauper

Born to a crowd in gold yet he died a pauper, a hermit
though of grave-digging stock, yet buried by vultures;
lived amongst priests; yet neither a dirge nor a feast
except for jackals who kept his vigil and a bee-line of dour
ants that marched in his drab and dank porch that neither
gave music nor mirth, yet while a pall of maggots draped

him, the fires in him crackled and joined the ether over
his flesh, in folds of that lowly soil, the lofty trees prayed
and welcomed a soul whose stomachs shall never again pain
of hunger, nor would rumbling thunder drone his yawning lips
for he shall no more pine for the leavings of rich grains
while the skirl of winds shut his eyes to envy and zips

his ears to swipes of poison lips, for he shall be lapped by waves
that'd cleanse his dishevelled state and all that he'd once craved.

## 22. Ebola

Damn your health warnings! Your state of emergencies
are beneath me; your quarantines, curfews, press releases
roadblocks and aid centres are all a piteous mockery!
How dare you bind me with your prayers? What effrontery!
I'm Ebola, the harbinger of death, and with this sharp sickle
I've severed handshakes, ritualistic burials and strangled
your laughter; I'm a prowling caution, your apprehension;
the respecter of no age, no religion, no profession...
The garish gowns of doctors neither amuse me
nor their masquerade cows me; your culling of bats,
your latex gloves, swipes and chlorine-baths don't move me.
Rams' blood at your portals doesn't sate my sinister wrath.
With pains of abscesses and nausea of corruption
I'll multiplied your poverty with wanton destruction...

## CLUSTER THREE:
Power and conflict

## 23. Cocoa Farmers

We're the cocoa farmers
the world's poorest
our cocoa buyers
the world's richest

we're the cocoa farmers
and what we farm
we do not eat
what we sell
we do not price

we're the cocoa farmers
our buyers do not haggle
and we do not argue
as we sellers are TAKERS
and our buyers are GIVERS

    we're the cocoa farmers
hundreds of years on, now fair traders
still trading as the world's poorest
still selling to the world's richest
still sellers of our rights
to price, to profit and power…

## 24. The Sermon of a Church Mouse

'As poor as a church mouse,' they say.
Point of correction: as poor as the congregation
because the money you saved on cigarettes
bought me tiles, sofas and comfy-carpets.
The money you saved on beer drinking
fetched me a fan to stop me from sweating.
The money you saved on cinemas and parties
bought me a palace and saved me from rabies.

'As poor as a church mouse,' they say.
Point of correction: as poor as the congregation,
while you emptied your house of food,
you stocked my store as often as you could.
While you starved yourself with fasting,
I nibbled, gnawed and gobbled to my bursting.
While you restrained from dating and fornication,
my family doubled your congregation


'As poor as a church mouse,' they say.
Point of correction: as poor as the congregation.
Thanks to your tithes, there is singing in my house,
thanks to your offering, there is dancing in my house,
thanks to your sowing of seeds, there is whistling in my house,
thanks to your pledges, there are playfights in my house,
thanks to your donation, there is jumping in my house.
God's good and all the time! In my house!

Njanguma S. Momodu

## 25. Godhead of Alafia

To the blood shed on altars
and slaughterhouses of Kuwait
blood of lambs laterally returned
to the bosom of Salone
blood on lips too drunk
on their dream of dollars
blood of my culled lambs
welcome to the godhead of Alafia…

To my silent ones whose soul shall
know no knell of church bells
but the report of guns
as your twenty-one-gun salute
to souls who shall know
no Columbia Davis or Virtues
but dollar bills as your embalmment
to all lost in action
but not lost in thoughts
welcome to the godhead of Alafia

For whom total annihilation
is your one minute silence
for whom there are neither
pallid faces nor weeping candles
but tears of toxic gases
welcome to the godhead of Alafia

to my silent lambs who shall know
no grave diggers and cremators
except the craters of landmines and missiles
for whom the dull chants of the Muslim Jamat

is replaced with a train
of pattering beads of blood
welcome to the godhead of Alafia

in the godhead of Alafia
o pious souls of lambs,
be exonerated
    blood of amputees
not on your head but upon
the heads of your cursed covens
    blood of soiled maidens
not on your hands but upon
the hands of cold commanders
    blood of the innocents
not on your heart but upon
the buyers of children
as bloodhounds of war
blood upon heads of sorcerers of amulets
blood upon the hands of chefs
lacing rice with antimony
blood upon the lips too drunk
on dreams of dollar
to sell you to silence....


1.    *Salone is a shorthand for Sierra Leone*

## 26. Commonwealth

What do you mean by the Commonwealth?
Is it where diseases and infant mortality is common
or where adult illiteracy and hand-to-mouth farming is common?
Is it where the masses live on zero or less than a dollar a day
or where the common wealth is in the hands of very few?

What do you mean by the common wealth?
Is it where English is the tenth language of the commons
or where the worship of the queen, as a goddess, is common?
Is it where the owners of oil do not price their products
or where turning peasants into conscripts is far too common?

What do you mean by the common wealth?
Is it where the huts, spices, mines and salt are taxed
or where the collected tax is not spent on the commons?
Is it where the people are too common to meet their queen
or where the rich live in the north and the poor in the south?

If the wealth is so common, why are the masses in rags?
If the masses are common, then where is the wealth?
Indeed, which of these is common: diamonds or diseases, rags or gold?
Which of these is wealthy: the palace, the parliament or the people?
What do you mean by the common wealth?

## 27. Wealth, the Creator of Poverty

On the first day, wealth chased off the farmers,
he smiled and nodded for creating dispossession.

On the second day, he bulldozed all rocks and trees,
scoured the land and made noise and fume pollution.

Next, with concrete and mortar he built skyscrapers,
pubs, gambling grounds all over his conurbation.

By night the allure of the city lights pulled swarms
of people that he'd later call mass migration.

He packed houses, hotels, hostels, the city streets,
culverts and created what he called dire congestion.

Then he created more jobs and over population
and to house everyone, he created deforestation.

With less jobs, less moneys in pockets and less food
to feed every mouth, he created mass malnutrition.

Unlike God who had a deserved rest on the seventh day,
He had to chase debtors and dared not talk of exhaustion.

Soon the farmers rose in bitter protest asking for their
compensation, crop rotation and green conservation.

But by day the traffic droned their hoarse protestation,
by night the city toffs took to the streets with intimidation.

## 28. The Question of Heaven

Is it true that it's tricky for the rich
to ever enter the gates of your kingdom?
What if he jumps off his high saddle,
offloads his camel, won't you let him in?

What if he turns buckets of sweat to gold,
didn't soil his hands with a pauper's blood?
What if he didn't bend his charge with switches,
didn't dock salaries, steal pensions or scrap grants?

What if he teaches unlucky hunters how to hunt,
covers the naked; pulls grovelling lips from gutters
to gains; is a mentor to the stray, father to orphans,
replaces tiny tin mugs, in begging hands, with corn seeds?

What if he draws pipe-borne water to the thirsty,
schools girls to escape the agony of forced marriages,
gives remedy to houses, chronically void of hope,
neither converts Alie's right to wrong nor covets his wife?

Would you flank your gates open and let him in your kingdom?

## 29. Rattitude

This rattitude started
by squashing our kind
to the likes of rats.

When the ratata of our guns
created the slum-rats of Sumalia
when the congealed blood
of the innocent divided
Gaza into enclaves and refugee camps
when ethnic cleansing
built road blocks in Sudan
when neglect shun its touch
on the squalors of kroo bay
that was when this rattitude started.

This rattitude will not end
while joblessness turns our nieces
into the favela rats of Brazil
while homelessness makes our boys
the culvert-toffs of San Pedro
while marginalisation push our cousins
to the remotest treehouses of Columbia.

This rattitude started
when Apartheid created
district four and the shanties of Njanga
when sorcery stilled
all blameless breaths in Haiti
when Jamaican gangs put
a virgin life in a wooden box
when hand grenades created
widows in Baghdad.

This rattitude will not end
while heroin and cocaine moulds
young supple lives into
the crackheads of Illinois
while opportunism vomits
pimps and prostitutes
while illiteracy spills into
a river of vulnerability
while prisons incubate
more burglars and suicides
while shelters breed
muddled minds for heartless shrinks….

This rattitude will not end
while AIDs and Ebola dress
in the guise of inoculation
while near-extermination makes
our uncles in Burundi carry
their lives on their heads
like snails carry their shells on their backs.
I know when this rattitude started
but wonder when it will end…

## 30. Kono People

We're a land of gems; they say, but why these beds of penury,
these rags, these singer beggars, these idle hands of
hopelessness?

Why are our houses razed and our shacks on the periphery
like condemned convicts or lepers bearing the hideousness
of an Abiku in the evil forest? Why are we in quarantine?

Why are we hurdled like slum rats whom the president
dare not greet? Why are we the untouchables, the Pharisees
the census dared not count and why are the powers hell-bent
on seeing us like the remains of plague victims in pan bodies?

Why must the sun shine darkness on our anxious eyes
and our trembling lips lament through rivers of wet faces
for the dead bodies on our pitted roads? Why the threats?
How long shall our voices pray for equality and peace?

Kono Leaders

Plucked from our ragged masses, you are now the guarded few
The flag has brushed up, bloated and suited in sleek brands.
You're the Hands they've groomed to dredge like mews
Jaws trained to kiss your kind for thirty carats of diamonds.

You're their undertakers. Lips that whisper in hushed voices
Eyes that wink and hand that gestures in ways of their white
house
You're the friends of men in purple gowns from the asphalt
roads
You're our bigwigs from roots with thin necks; you're our
bloated
Bosses

they've taught to be bringers of bulldozer and the kimberlite
but not the razers of houses and crusher of our day-dreams
granted
they've thought you to be the bringers of caterpillars and dynamites
but not the causer of noise, floods, broken hopes and esteems
granted
they've taught you to be the bringer of the roads and prosperity
but not the bringer of potholes, mosquitoes, debt and depravity?
Granted.

*1. Pan-body: is a shack made of metallic zinc or flattened oil drums.*

## 31. Thank God My Daddy Is Not Poor

Thank God my daddy is not poor
as we don't have to sleep outdoors

he works nightshifts to pay uncle landlord
copper coins for me and tithes for our God

He'd rather borrow to pay our school fees,
works three jobs, to pay our feeding money

rather do overtime than steal or beg
does odd jobs or ask me to sell boiled eggs.

He pays his osusu to make big, big money
like the one you win on a bomber lottery

thank God my daddy is not poor
as we don't have to sleep outdoors.


1. *Bomber lottery: is a windfall win or a rollover on a lottery*

## 32 Tax Slave

Dear Alienus,

Is it true that you want to come to earth to relax?
Too bad! Cos earth's as noisy and smoky as hell
for unlike Mars, where water's free; earth's TAX
TAX, TAX! It's tax to buy and tax to sell.

We've V.A.T on air, on water and death
Tariff on rice, advalorem on oil
We've Excise on butter and cigarettes
and our P.AY..E rarely rewards our toils.

Just as congestion charge's a noose in every town
so's Green tax a poison on our petrol and diesel
Just as Road tax disembowels us, like vicious hounds
ripping their quarry, so it drowns us in toll charges.

Here, we've higher charges or high rates
or sky high prices or mean fees
Here, we've hidden war tax or zero rebates
or surcharged duties or reduced annuity.

Corporation tax's sward that beheads our profits
Council tax's a bullets that breaches our houses
stamp-duty's a chamber that gases buyers of bedsits
inheritance tax's a stake that impale us and our spouses.

It's TAX TAX TAX till we're grey and wax
so stay on Mars; as we, on earth, do not relax
because we earthlings live to pay mansion tax.

Your one and only friend,
Earthly Tax-slave.

## 33. Tsunami Monday (14.08.17 the landslide disaster in Sierra Leone)

Farewell, o sealed lips
now sworn to silence
hearts that never dreamt
your procession to be
a train of fetid waters, farewell.
Farewell o stealthy feet
that never imagined
your careful crossing of thresholds
could reduce our smiles
our strengths, our numbers, farewell.
Farewell to minds
that never imagined
an eclipse in a Monday dawn
never imagined your dirges
as demented blues of gushing winds
reminiscent of cotton fields, farewell.
Never imagined your prayers
as wails of thunder
your sermons
as a rumbling firmament, farewell.
    Farewell to hands
too stiff to pen their wills
To minds too inert
to imagine a wreckage of houses
the rubble of landslides
as their grave, farewell
    Farewell to souls now free
of sweat on wrinkled brows
immune to mocking lips and gloating eyes
Farewell.

Farewell to eyes
now shut on the pallid face

of high heavens
ears cocked
to rooster's crow and alarm bells
Farewell to our fallen garden
Farewell to pain, to fear, to waiting…
Farewell. Farewell farewell...

## 34. Harmattan

I'm the camel that gulps your well till it's empty
the grunt in your guts, the bubbles in your slushy acid
and like creases and scars, I paint you with poverty
iron your intestines like your pocket until they're torrid

Your cosy jumpers neither make me less Antarctic
nor your laments of squandering last year's harvest
stops me from leeching you till you're anorexic
and, like Brima, chide you till you learn to invest.

Excuse me if I've lean your skin and taut your ribs
or scribbled tide marks of wrinkles over your sunken eyes.
Too bad that I can neither help cracking your lips nor fib
about not failing your crops or letting your cattle die.

*1. A mythical spirit of the sea that visits the land righting people's wrongs but not before flogging them. The soirit then disappears into thin air.*

**CLUSTER FOUR**
Taking a stand

## 35. Counting Down the Steps Out of Poverty

Dearest son, here are my steps into wealth:
always be an employer that keeps all his profit. TEN

Being an employee must always be temporary
to gain skills: for an employee's pay is survival pay. NINE

Don't slave for money; rather, let money slave for you. EIGHT

Note that money's a stranger; so get well acquainted
and remember to to play the good, over-protective host.
SEVEN

Investment in skills and college education is not a waste but an
asset. SIX

No unsecured loans means zero bad debts and
ploughing profit back makes business grow. FIVE

Always treat yourself out of excess savings
such as moneys saved from reduced expenditure. FOUR

Less debtors lessens risks; less creditors lessen liabilities.
THREE

Be disciplined and savvy and don't be fazed by either failure
nor swiping lips that call you a scrooge, just focus on your goal.
TWO

Remember the indignities of poverty and let it stir you up the
rung of success

be sure footed as you climb saying 'no' to failure, 'no' to a fall
and 'No' to the gutters. ONE

Religiously obey all these warnings and poverty shall be a thing of the past in your world of wealth. ZERO.

## 36. Spirit of a Family Home

Out of the shrapnel of bullets
I rise over the putrid gutters of war...
out of the subterranean soil
I rise past the stench, to see shovels
clearing the squalor
out of the ashes of woods
I rise as a wall with ears strained
to my children's ideals....

You might have intoxicated
my children on a brandy of fear
but I, who have surged up
through the wretched maze of earth
enraptured by the zest of rebuilders,
rise like ants
in the wake of earthquakes
moulding clay into anthills
rise with the claws
of foxes scraping into forms
rise with the nimbleness
of rats burrowing into holes
rise with dreams
of snakes coiling in comfort,
rise out of pulverised blocks
to mutate into rafters
shielding my children
from the fiercest elements.

Out of the grains of nails
I rise as windows letting in
whirls of opportunities
out of the powdery rags
I rise as doors to usher in
hugs, kisses and handshakes

like the harp, of the aquamarine realm
that summons her shoal of salmons
to a diurnal dance
I too rise
as an inchoate voice
calling for a keepsake
these unfurled buds of peace
saying hush to mouths too hasty
to sell the family loom
I rise as a spark
of tolerance and sacrifice
to greed-drunken minds
too replete with fears of free riders
out of piggy-banks and joint-hands
I rise in a stern voice against hearts
too rash to call me the tower of babel
I rise, I rise as the spirit of the family home…

## 37. Alamɔry

Wɛn Alamɔry bang, na 4 tarwar
Tinap! Dɛp di add-up ɛn di yargbah
Nor tɛllɛh, mi man, na 4 ɔl sɔrbɔh
Eat dafiri, mi man, managɛ thɛ yɛbbɔh

Way u bɛllɛh di tɔk, na 4 tinap
Do Ajibu Jallɔh, 4 byɛ onɛ butter-cup
Benda butik, 4 wan candlɛ ɛn kɛrɔsɛnɛ
Hustle from Congo cross to Magazine

Way Alamɔry bang, u nor 4 takɛ gun
ɔr dɔ 419 ɔr jigɔlɔ ɔr Larry ɛn bit gɔn
Nɔr majalaji ɔr gambul ɔr rɔn tɔ ɔmɔlay
ɔr yɔu gɔ lɔɔk cracɛ pass Pitiparay

Wɛn thɛ bɛllɛh grɔnbull, sɔmɛ di lɛf thɛ kɔntri
Sɔm di axɛ jujuman, 'paa makɛ mi gɛntri!'
But Sam, way u pray 2 Gɔd, nɔr fɔrgɛt 4 tri
Bɛcɔs if u nɔr tri add, u pɔckɛt gɔ dri

Mi man, Alamɔry nɔr sabbi agɛ and ɛducation
Mi sister Alamɔry nɔr sabbi cɔmplɛxion
Alamɔry nabba nɔ gɛnda ɛn rɛligion
Alamɔry nabba nɔ tribɛ and rɛgion

Sɔ nɔr tɛllɛh, mi brɔda, nar fɔr ɔl sɔbɔh
Nɔr bit gɔn ɔɔh, mi sistɛr, na fɔr managɛ thɛ yɛbbɔh

ɛ = E
ɔ = O

## 38. Poverty, You Have Failed

Poverty, you've failed
because the soul of my yawning mouth
craves not for a food that taunts
but yearns for that solitude
beneath the ribs
thirsts not
after the comfort
of your drinks that derides
but carols of its longing
for the feel of a tender finger
stubbed to the lips
that doesn't goad.

Neither moan
nor whimper
but chants of its oath of silence
that doesn't jeer
neither shudder
nor clatter
nor explode with expletives
that chaffs or stiffen with grief;
rehearses the eternal silence
of a peace that once knew no hunger.

Poverty you've failed
because the soul of an empty hand
bunches not in vengeance
but squeezes a liquid hymn
of its longing for days
beneath the lungs
longing for those fingers
that once clenched unto their peace
of the womb in a world

where no one groped
in your sneering eclipse
sings of a palm spread open
not like the tin mugs
of singer beggars
but like a furled lotus leaf
soothed by the fans
of the harmattan of peace.

Poverty you've failed
for the soul of the naked body
pines not after your delusions
of clothes but intones
of its wish for the security
of the ammonitic fluid free of gems
vices and heartaches
serenades of days
when the soul neither recoiled
in shame nor shielded behind
a crestfallen face
but thirsts for a peace once relished
in that sphere of no care
swaddled in its duvet of innocence

Poverty you've failed
for the soul of a flaccid stomach
lusts not, after your transient food
but croons of the bliss of days
when its navel was once joined
to its mother's
sings of season of ambience
free of the pang of hunger
free of the growls of want
filled to bursting
with contented peace.

Poverty you've failed
because the soul of the sunken eyes
drools not after
your deceitful banquet
but sings of days
of sightless tranquillity
blind to envy and jealousy
longs for the days
of a blank mind
of a foetal life, free of wrath
greed, wiles and other deadly sins
longs for the quietude
of the sentient sod of peace.
Indeed, poverty you've failed.

## 39. When Shall We Make Poverty History?

When shall we make poverty history?

When distrust isn't the highlight
of each day.
When flowers either replace
the guns of gang or hugs and handshakes
replace the knives of thieves.
When eyes are blind to vices
noses refuse to sniff cocaine and veins stiffen
against the prick of syringes of heroin.
When girls are not sold
like heifers on stalls of immorality
and desperation finds the heart
too sanitised to spread its contagion.

We make poverty history
when the eyes see life
as God's and the conscience warns
the hand against its wilful snuffing
of breath out of the nostrils.
When neither the voice
      of the mind calls its owner stupid
      nor the conscience thinks
      of the heart as lazy.
When neither the feet sidle
      off from school bells
nor the heart dump pens in bins.

When shall we make poverty history?

When the ears unfailingly strain
to rants of a distraught heart
the communal hand offers
potions to mend a bilious spleen.

When the wide arm
of the village embraces
the stray legs back to the fold
of the human family…
       when employers see
sisters in their workers
the soul lingers to see life
fulfilled and not living:
from hand-to-mouth.

We make poverty history
when factories neither exhale fumes
nor the jaws of the earth gobble
up vile waste
when our oceans are
 not congealed with tarry oil
nor an earth bare of its green hair
nor see breaches
in the ozone of the sky.


When shall we make poverty history?

When the mind knows
his left from right
the jaws have rice
and the heads have rafters.
When the back is laid
with cloth and wise minds
counsels mindless hearts.
When the pains of one heart
is not the smile of another's face.
when a hand dared not sell its conscience.

We make poverty history
when earthquakes can
neither break the heart
nor the blows of trauma
or diseases cow the mind.
When neither the Jones's gold
tinges the eyes with envy
nor the tongues drool
after its neighbour's wife
when vicious circle of rags,
of old, is halted.
That is when we make poverty history!

# CLUSTER FIVE
Enlightenment

## 40. The Maths of Poverty

80% of the world's wealth, they say
belongs to 20% of the richest.
What uneven distribution!
What multiplication of malnutrition!
What disproportionality! What disparity!

20% of the world's wealth, they say
belongs to 80% of the world.
What polarization between
Rich and Poor; what poverty
In wealth; what wealth in poverty!
What magnification of misery!
What extrapolation of penury!


If half of the poorest people's share
went in ONE POCKET, what greed!
What slice of hunger!
what quantification of fragments
what decimation of generations
what recurrence of frustration.

If sex sold films and vices sold
books, what was the probability
of wars selling guns?
High! And selling
Innocent lives? High!

If gun, like flowers,
covered the earth
what was the probability
of turning our Eden
into enclaves? High!

into refugee camps? High!

If only 10% of charity funds
is what trickles to the needy
what subtraction of lives
what substitution of greed
for lives! What elimination
of happiness!

If the north paid
her jobless
while the south
starved his jobless
what elimination
of happiness!

If the north helped
her disabled
while the south
impoverished his
disabled. How acute!
How biased! How obtuse.

Out of the rubble
of northern wars
a train of rationers
a tower of food banks.
Out of the bequest
of the south, an IMF loan,
a circle of corruption.
Barns emptied
to fund court cases
what acrimonious harem
what an ever increasing
vicious circle; what a

circumference of evil

Show me the annual food waste
of a country in the north
and I'll show you
500,000 tons of weight.
I'll show you Mount Everest
a thousand whales
three thousand Asian elephants

Show me fifty tons
of supermarkets' wasted food
and I'll show you
£50 million pounds
spent on landfilled sites
on incineration
I'll show you pollution
ten million churning stomachs
that could have been hushed
ten million skeletal children
that could have been fed
how many schools
it could've built
how many illiterates
it could've educated
how many homeless
it could've sheltered
how many school fees
it could've paid
how many malaria vaccines
it could have bought!

## 41. Poverty

I'm not a killer as you think
rather I'm a teacher;
the feet
that lead your soul down dark
dungeons of depravity
the finger
that clicks shut your fleshy eyes
and gives sight to your inner world
to see beyond the obvious
but do you see me
as the trainer of your soul?

I'm not a miser as you think
yes, I do empty your pocket
not a jingle of coins
not a shuffle of notes
but in that flatness of your pocket
thread meshes with thread
uniting fabric to fabric
in a family reunion of cloths
but do you see me
as a joiner of families?

I'm not as greedy as you think
because in the empty pocket
of the wise
I plant a seed
of detachment from gold
and the emptiness of the palm
at birth and death.
In the empty pocket
of a fool, he sees me
for the greed in his eyes

sees me for deprivation
when will you not see me
for desperation and
powerlessness?

I'm not as wicked as you think
because to the wise
an empty stomach returns
him to contentment of its cradle
in the womb, the emptiness plods
his hand to fend; to claim oneness
with the starved, the prophets
and the saints.
I empty the stomach
of a fool and he hears me
for the churns of his stomach
when will he stop seeing me
for the twinges of his hunger?

I poke the skin
through a rag of the wise
and he sees me for humility
his days of nakedness
under the ribs
but to a fool
I'm his mist of shame
his gutter of battered esteem
when will he ever listen
to my whisper and learn
rather than see me
as his reason to envy
the finery of the gentry?

## 42. The Soul Man

After the continent of selfishness
far beyond the country of envy
I crossed the city of greed
on sprinted heels detouring
the district of sloth
and dodging the town
of wrath until I entered
a lowly village
of altruism where
I chanted with
the Soul-man.

From the streets of gluttony
I trudged on…
picked my way across
the road of pride
until I reached that
notorious cul-de-sac
all drowned in a saucy lust
and other vices
which drove me
to that smallest avenue
of humility in that precinct
of contentment
within a cellar of the last house
of a close, where I prayed with
the Soul-man.

Beyond the hills of prejudice
in that valley where
the mind is one with the heart
where nature, like man,
is all blind to the differences

of skin tone, gender, disability
tongues, faiths and age
and at a table all teemed with souls
levitating above avarice
I took a chair beside
the Soul-man.

Off the grand mansion
of selfishness
beyond the costal sea
of envy and greed
above the hand-made cars
and designer clothes
in the lowly bed of altruism
chants the Soul-man.

In the tiniest continent of peace
across mounts of pride
in the smallest country of humility
at the heart of the puniest district
of contentment
and in the pious town of love
cheers the Soul-man.

In an ornate study, stocked with books
on oneness with nature
at a table teemed with souls
levitating
beyond shades of skins,
tongues, genders, disability
ages and faiths,
chairs the Soul-man.

## 43. Lightmare

O contented fire in my mortal soul
the shade that soothes me from
the oppressive heat of the red sun
how can I ever thank you?

Ever present light that never sets
the hand that feeds my mouth
when the greedy sun starves
my stomach
the wand that blinds
my fleshy eyes
when the red sun beckons
with its allure of envy and jealousy
how can I ever praise you?
I can but only bow in your praise.

Soft tissue to my pallored eyes
soothing whispers of consolation
in time of leaden grief
how can I ever thank you?

For when the looming sun idles
my hands, you make me the Adam
of your Eden
weeder of weeds; pruner of petals
of love, and in your praise, o giver of hope,
I've fenced off your orchard against
Vanity, Gluttony, Wrath, Avarice
and Deceit.
How do you like it?

How can I ever thank he
who consoles me in myriad ways?

In the drought of a harmattan
that singes my lips, you soothe
my addled mind
key to my parched, pitted desert
oasis to the malevolent dots
on my skin, you're the ultimate cure
to my gnarled trees
you give lushness
to the swivelled trunks
of my fruit trees, you're a succulent sap
to my bland, pitted plot
you're a moisture and a rich loam.
How can I ever praise you?
I can but only bow in your praise.

       You're my consolation
for when, like roaches, bats and snakes
I'm isolated from the allure of the day,
you hold me in the fold of your fireside
grip me with your stories that recount:
no shallow pulses, no gulping throats
no sunken eyes writhing with anguish
no ragged souls grovelling in squalor
no heart battered beyond repair
feebly beating its last drums
       but you rally me with words
of a peace within, set with wings, feet,
fins, in unison, pulsing with your
breath of harmony; entranced by the
heat of peace, the echo of wholeness.

You're my consolation
when the sledgehammer of the sun
shatters my heart, you hold me
in your vice
heat me with your forge of fire

and wrought me into a titanium of peace
pain-proof for eternity.
O light of light within
that saves me from the mare of day,
how can I thank you? I can but only bow
in your praise; forever in your praise!

# CLUSTER SIX
Motivation and Nature

## 44. Songs of the Southern Stoics

Out of the slums that christened us
as beggars and tramps of the streets
we rise in thunderous barks that cow
cut-throats from courts and cul-de-sacs.

Out of the wounds of isolation, we rise
as souls of the great hyenas to stand up
against the frowning face of the city.

Out of the inventive paws of coyotes
we rise to mould couches out of coarse
verandas, make kennels out of cooking cinders
and harmattan-beds out of warm ashes.

Out of the loyalty of the great hounds
in our resilient soul, up and up
we rise out of our castrations
as fierce eunuchs to gather a flock
like a hundred men put together
with wags of stubby tails- in greetings-
we thank the Dane in us
for ingratiating us at our lord's orders.

Out of the smell sense of jackals we rise
to outlived curses, whips, kicks and stones
rise to sniffed out rabbits from their warren,
to hush the vacuous cries of empty pots
and fill the hollowed whimper
in our lords' stomachs; we rise!

Out of the wolves of the canine valleys
within us, we rise with our ears strained
to the songs of our sworn secrets of hope

rise with sights that see beyond evil
rise with a smell sense to perceives death
rise on limbs that trek the streets of toffs
rise with strengths a vagrants by day
and the intuition of sentries by night.

Out of the crack of whips
of our cash-strapped lords
our paws pray for a quell
to the booming bark
of retaliation within us
 we rise to the call
of tried and tested patience
in our adaptive soul
 we rise and soothe
our mouths, long denied of the fattest
of wildebeests as we breakfast
on stale leftovers
for out of the burnt crusts of rice

we rise out
of skeletal ribs of hunger
rise to the fate that condemned us
to feed on faeces without utterance of scorn.

O let the waves say how neglect once clothed
us in ticks and rabies
 how hardship once cowed
our gnashed teeth to grovel at the very feet
that kicked us
 stoop to the very hand
that hauled stones at us
prostrate to the very lips
that once spluttered curses at us
soused us out of sight and reach.

Growls of the Great Danes, within us,
cowed by man's rods, squashed by poverty,
unsheathe your ferocious fangs and gather
your broken pack on the prairie of our hearts.
Within the socket of our hollowed faces
rise with a third eye that glares at ghosts
with your thunderous roar
that thwarts the entry of wizards
into our owners' ordered lives
Rise! Rise! Rise!

## 45. Rich and Poor

The rich and poor
might think
themselves strong
but not as strong
as a crawling tortoise
that carries its house
on its back and yet
lives longer than both.

The rich and poor
might think
themselves the fastest
but not as swift as a fly
that lives for eight
happy days
and gladly dies.

An Inuit might sleep
on a bed of ice in her igloo
and the richest man might
snore on his memory foam
in his mansion
but dreams visit both.

The Korowai busman
might brave a fall
to climb his tree house
and the rich man's pocket
might afford him
the dearest penthouse
but both must share
that panoramic view.

The rich man's wardrobe
might contain the choicest of labels
and a poor man's wardrobe
might contain a rack of rags
but none is as poised
and confident as a peacock
in his suit made
to suit for life.

The rich might fast
during the thirty days
of Ramadan and eat at sunset
and the poor might fast
during the forty days of lent
and eat at sunset;
but the snail beats both
by fasting during
the whole of the harmattan.

The rich man's pantry
might burst its seams with food
and the poor man's store
might be sparse with grains of rice
but both must feed
the flies, rats and worms
that will one day feed on them.

## 46. If

If you can hold up when Leones fail
to shuffle in your pocket
resolve to plod on when your degrees fail
to translate into gainful jobs
feel frustration but not make rejections
your goddess; push pass dejection
and never let the successes of the Jones'
run you into the ground
forge on with head and shoulders high
always keeping up your guard
till the rain clouds clear and shine
on the full ripening of your destiny
inspiring is your type of candour
worthy of our emulation.

If you can hawk the whole of Wellington
with wares set on your head
neck squashed in but unbroken
by a load twice your body weight
unfazed by ogling eyes, yet laugh
off wolf whistles and cat cries
sing when the blast of uptown bars
drone out your call to customers
yet neither lament nor curse your lot
when traders choose other vendors
over you and not begrudge them
but tighten your girdle and trek on
from RowCooper, Congo Cross to Magazine…
empowering is your type of model
worthy of our emulation.

If you can stay steadfast when the honey
laced tongues of shrines lure
with promises of gold; be tempted

but ditch the broad-way of temptation
neither moved by ill-gotten wealth
nor be a party to cads, toffs and gangs
but toe the lonely path of contentment
with its small measures of fortunes
and not be distraught by the dying
in waiting, the uncertainty and flukes
your highlight of life is a fervour
of patience worthy of our emulation.

If you can keep your honour
when all about you is replete with vices
yet not make indignity your chaperone
but remain chaste in Gomorrah
unyielding to empty promises
undaunted by taunts for your prudish stance
and not follow the beckoning finger of evil
but consider your derailment
as a scandal, a betrayal, a plague,
a spectre that haunts your generation
honourable is your standard
that's worthy of our emulation.

1. *Leones: currency of Sierra Leone*

## 47. A Song of a Southern Son

O sweet sweltering, southern sun
when shall your morrow's dawn
vanquish mortality in our infancy
and clear the eclipse of illiteracy?

    When shall your sons
grow into great fathers
who can read bed-time stories
to their daughters
and when shall your daughters
grow into great mothers
who can teach a whole nation
to be peacemakers?

Can't wait to see
the dawn of that day
when your streets
are cleared of hawking children
sweatshops and brothels
cleared of slaving children
dustbins and culverts
cleared of vagrant children
ritualist altars
cleared of sacrificial children.

O sweet sweltering, southern sun
when shall your morrow's dawn
turn a day's sweat into a dollar
and when shall your tea
be priced by its owners
your daughter's dowry
not paid at eight
your son's life not used
to test weapons and plagues.

### Njanguma S. Momodu

Can't wait to see
the dawn of that day
when the gaps between
gold and rags is no more
and the living from
hand-to-mouth is no more
and the disease of
cap in hand is no more
and the ailment of debt
is long gone…

## 48. Lullaby

Take heart, my friend, when nature sadly impairs
your speech, your hearing, your sight and mobility.
Take heart when evil wiles and politics prices you
out of a job, when your brain fails to get desired results.

Take heart, my friend, when you're born to a house
full of vices: harlots, gamblers, thieves and drunks.
When fate fails you in your claim of oneness with equals
see these factors as your lot that moulds your character.

Take heart, my friend, when you're made an orphan
fostered or adopted, when destiny condemns you to
a life of squalor and grime, see these factors as your lot
to make the dysfunctional as functional as you can.

Take heart, my friend, when you're made a statistic,
a victim of circumstance, when your justice is denied,
your dearest turns into a foe, when your chances are blighted
and when your offers are shunned; never resign to fate…

Take heart, my friend, when you're the lone voice
in a crowd, when you're an island unto yourself.
Learn to be an expert of challenges, accept your fate
and make contentment, humility and action your friends.

## 49. They're Not Our God

Brothers, let's rest assured of only this:
that cronyisn and nepotism aren't our God
that greed will not have his evil wishes
that neither threats nor wiles will drown us
for envy and jealousy are not our God.

Neither rags of slumps nor pains of penury
shall put our lips to the chalice of corruption
while selfishness denies us our rightful share
of our nation's china and crush us with Alamory
because they're neither our fate nor our God.

Sisters, let's rest assured of only this:
that neither wizard nor the snob is our God
neither flaunting of clothes, cars and fat purses
will neither dull our resolve nor erase our bliss
never reduced to bones as hard as baked sods.

They'll neither blot out our talent nor conceal
our fate, neither condemn us to singer-beggars
nor make us suffer their malevolent ordeals
of chained slaves to heartless employers.
I assure you, once more, that they're not our God.

1.  *Alamory: krio slang for hardship.*

**CLUSTER SEVEN**
Human Conditions

## 50. Hunger

No jingling coins to buy me ingredients
no rustling notes to buy me some rice
and the room of my stomach lays vacant
and Hunger rapped, at my door, twice!

Urgent like a patter of rain, he banged
so I let him in, with all his vices and rashness
but vile, like a living-in landlord, he raged
as his thundering music drowned my calmness

I braced the walls to hem his nuisance in
but he notched up his sound to a deafening din…

A gulp of water neither sated nor calmed him
my finest suit neither dignified nor hid him
my strolls in streets neither distracted nor coaxed him
all the while that I trekked, I carried him…

Now a tongue of fire like a man in a race
he boiled my skin and drenched me with sweat
he dried my lips, slowed my pace, drew my face
and took me up dizzying heights to see his beat

'Feed me!' he chided, 'Tell of me and beg,'
he dared me, but for that tiny voice in me
my pride, my contentment, wouldn't let me.
'Steal for me,' he pleaded, 'or die, believe me!'
but the angel of morals in me, wouldn't let me.

Yes! The food did come, but not after my faint
to be rallied by rice from Samaritans and saints
my hands punched him and feet sent him asunder
as he fled for dear life, away from my fire of anger.

Wish he'd gone, but in the pleading eyes of maids
I see him
In the cracked voice of a singer- beggar
I hear him
In the sun-beaten face of a madman
I see him
In the babbling laments of a pedestrian
I hear him

Lining the skeletal ribs of a dog, he's alive
In the hollowed eyes of a widow, he's alive
In the pallid shade of an orphan, he's alive
In a child's tantrum and in her mother's quarrels
he's alive; he's SADLY alive…

## 51. Poverty is Not a Crime

Poverty, they say, is not a crime.
Really? So why not sing that to civil servants
who've had to complement their pay with bribes.

Poverty, they say, is not a crime.
Really? So why not sing that to city cut-throats
who've had to rob, kill and swindle to survive.

Poverty, they say, is not a crime.
Really? So why not sing that to prisoners
who've had to make a debtors' jail their home.

Poverty, they say, is not a crime.
Really? So why not sing that to the homeless
who've had to rough it on streets for not paying their rent.

Poverty, they say, is not a crime.
Really? So why not sing it to victims of the slumps
the dropouts, jobless, drunks, prostitutes and suicides.

Poverty, they say, is not a crime; really?

## 52. Poverty - an Armed Robber

Your gloved hands picked my lock
and out flew my security, my serenity.
Why poverty? Why

empty my wardrobe of dignity
and left me in rags of harassment.
Why poverty? Why

empty my store of food, my tuck shop of wares
and left my pocket and stomach empty.
Why poverty? Why

put a cold steel to my head, startle me
with your balaclava, your stern stare.
 Why poverty? Why

drench me with sweat, clothe me in fear
and make me grovel at your feet.
Why poverty? Why

trash my house with violence and frustration,
left my mind in a muddle, my heart in palpitation.
Why poverty? Why

pinch my voice, hollow my eyes, crack my lips,
dull my heartbeat and chase off my laughter.
Why poverty? Why

clad in swarthy cloak like the slayer with a sickle
and trail me like a shadow that throttles the neck.
Why poverty? Why? Why?

## 53. The Man-Eater of the South

The north said to the south
what is poverty like?
And the south said:

It's a drowning throat
gulping in the channels
dodging the grizzly, arched
back of embarrassment.
It's a giant man
coiled, crescent,
in the guts of a luggage
recoiling from a sniffer dog
from the prying eyes of x-rays…
it's an eye burrowing
in its sockets, sidling away
from sides of a malevolent mouth
curled backward
baring curved ivory fangs
that devours.

It's sweat-shone biceps
digging the earth
a finger poised with a pen
to bury the pangs of hunger
to keep bailiffs and landlords
at bay.

It's like grime
chasing off cleanliness
like squalor
chasing off healthiness
like rust
chasing off the steely toughness

like a leech
sucking the skin dry of sheen
like time
wringing youth out of life

it's a greedy ghost
dislodging the stomach of its juices
eating coins
out of pockets
emptying notes
 out of accounts
gnawing at the heart
of confidence
gobbling esteem,
whole!
Bagging laughter
from the dimples of the face
etching the face
of its simple smiles

like a plague
inundating the shanties
pouting mouths
writhing eyes

breaking springs in legs
clogging up veins,
shrinking up arteries
marking every face
with a scarlet letter

like a cell
hiving lives on remand
manacling hands and feet
quarantined
denied visits

and food and privileges
uncertain of charges
or court hearing or release date

it's the man eater of the South.

## Poems: one, or two, line summary

The Hawker: looks at how poverty instigates child labour and the consequences on children's lives.
Diamond Diggers: looks at diamond digging as a fantasy; an escape from poverty and the impacts of diamond mining on health and the environment.
Pills of Pa Kumasi: looks at the fatalistic effects of poverty; particularly how it breeds hopelessness leading to suicide.
Death of a Doctor: looks at the impact of poverty on people's aspirations.
Usain Bolt in Sierra Leone: looks at the impact of poverty on the nutritional and academic preparation in a competitive world.
The Pride of Pa Palma: looks at the show of resilience in the face of abject poverty.
The Beggar: looks at the impact of poverty on the victims of war.
The Phantom of Fasting: looks at poverty as a phase of life or experience taking the soul through hardship to attain enlightenment.
Bra Samora and His Stiletto Shoe: looks at poverty as a symbolism and as an extended metaphor of testing the loyalty of love in adverse situations.
The Prodigal Son: looks at wasteful governance and its impact on poor people.
Bra Bockarie and His Sack of Rice: looks at the psychological impact of poverty on future relationships.
The Widow Who Married Her Church: looks at the impact of poverty on cultural and religious loyalties.
The Soul Whisperer: looks at the harshness of life and failed dreams.
The Man Who Sold Himself off on a Loan: looks at the impact of poverty on relationships and as an instigator of resignation and hopelessness.
The Hypocrite: looks at the psychological impact of poverty such as self-hatred.

Cookies to Heaven: looks at the psychological impact of poverty in terms of envy and jealousy

Dodger: looks at dodging fares in the global north as a thrill in contrast to dodging fares in the global south as a necessity of life.

Chimney: looks at the self-destructive aspects of poverty.

Job: looks at man's doom and sense of hopelessness in the face of an indefatigable effort of devotion.

Poverty Projects: looks at the tenacity of the poor to rise to challenging times or hardship.

Funeral of a Pauper: looks at poverty as the root cause of marginalisation within communities.

Ebola: looks at man's vulnerability to plagues how they compound poverty.

Cocoa Farmer: looks at the powerlessness of farmers in the bargaining game.

The Sermon of a Church Mouse: looks at the role of religious institutions in perpetuating poverty.

The Godhead of Alafia: looks at the enlisting of child soldiers in world conflicts as an escape from poverty.

Commonwealth: questions the benefits of the commonwealth to the third world countries.

Wealth, the Creator of Poverty: looks at the conflict between wealth creation and the reduction of human comfort and destruction of the environment.

The Question of Heaven: questions whether it's wealth per se, good deeds or station in life that determines entry into heaven.

Rattitude: looks at man's inhumanity to man and the consequences of poverty.

Kono People: looks at abject poverty in a land that is endowed with diamonds and great brains.

Thank God my Dad Is Not Poor: looks at a child's notion of poverty.

Tax Slave: looks at the damming effects of taxation on the lives of people.

Tsunami Monday: looks at the disastrous effects of a landslide on the lives of the community and how it leaves the poor worst off.
Harmattan: looks at the impact of the seasons on the lives of the poor.
Counting Down the Steps Out of Poverty: looks at the proactive steps to take out of the shackles of poverty.
Spirit of a Family Home: looks at a family home as a symbol of family unity galvanising against disunity and poverty.
Alamory: looks at the spirit of resilience in the face of abject penury.
Poverty, You've Failed: looks to the ambience and the contentment of the past – in the womb - for strength to fight poverty.
When Shall We Make Poverty History?: is a rallying call to fight to eradicate all forms of poverty.
The Maths of Poverty: looks at the causes of the widening gap between the rich and the poor.
Poverty: looks at the schooling of the soul through suffering.
Soul-Man: looks at detachment as a coping strategy in abject poverty.
Lightmare: looks at the use of the inner courage to cope with the outer realities of poverty.
Songs of the Southern Stoics: looks at poverty from a dog's point of view.
Rich and Poor: looks at how both the rich and poor fair worst against the powers of nature, suggesting that the rich and poor are different only materially but equal in their fears and weaknesses.
If: praises the numerous efforts of men and women in arduous conditions and draws motivation from them.
A Song of a Southern Son: sings of the hopeful anticipation to the end of poverty.
Lullaby: gives encouragement to all that find themselves in adverse situations.
They're Not Our God: celebrates the spirit of survival.

Njanguma S. Momodu

## About the Author

**Njanguma Momodu** was Born in 1968, at Bumii (Tongo - Air fields) in the Eastern Province of Sierra Leone – West Africa. Njanguma, or big, sleek and smart cat with forty-seven lives, was truly sleek in his blue uniform in 1976 when he enrolled at the Roman Catholic Primary School. From there, he entered KSS (Koidu Secondary School) in 1983 and showed that he was truly smart when he completed his secondary school in 1988. In July of that same year, he transformed himself from a domestic cat into a big cat by flying to London. From 1988-1995, he studied Business, Law and Economics at the Kilburn Polytechnic and, in 2000, he entered the University of Westminster and graduated four years later with an honours degree in Business Studies. Shortly afterwards, he undertook a post-graduate degree at the Institute of Education - University of London. It was while studying at these various institutions that he discovered the elixir to prolong his life, and what better way to earn himself these forty-seven lives than to write poems and stories.

So, as a true leopard with writing all over him, Njanguma published some poems in 'M'frique' in 'On the Threshold of a Dream' next there was 'Roots' in 'The Best Poems of 1995' (both published by the North American Library). Five poems were also published in the Feather Books Publication and 'Bless You O Tireless Hand' was published by 'Still life.' Other publications include: a collection of fables and myths for children called 'The five Fingers' 2012 and his gothic collection of short stories called 'Daughter of Albino' was published in 2015.

Njanguma Momodu is a Founder, Manager of 'Tailored

Tuition' a tuition centre which prepares learners for 11 and 13+ English exams for both private and grammar schools. The centre also prepares secondary school learners for their GCSE English, Business and Economics exams. Njanguma lives in London. He is married and have four children.

www.ingramcontent.com/pod-product-compliance
Lightning Source LLC
Chambersburg PA
CBHW032141040426
42449CB00005B/343